HOW TO START A
CAR WASH
BUSINESS

A Comprehensive Guide to Opening, Running and
Growing Your Own Automobile Washing Business

TOMMY PARHAM

TABLE OF CONTENTS

INTRODUCTION

"How to Start a Car Wash Business" is a comprehensive manual designed to help aspiring entrepreneurs enter the lucrative world of car wash. Whether you're an auto enthusiast looking to turn your passion into a profitable venture or a business-minded individual seeking a new opportunity, this book provides the essential knowledge and practical advice you need to launch and manage a successful car wash business.

With the automotive industry's increasing demand for professional car care services, starting a car wash business can be a rewarding and lucrative venture. However, the path to success requires more than just a love for cars. This book takes you through every step of the journey, from understanding the intricacies of car wash to developing a solid business plan and establishing a strong brand presence.

In this book, you'll learn how to identify your target market, analyze the competition, and position your business for success. You'll discover the essential equipment and supplies needed to deliver top-notch wash services and gain insights into hiring and training skilled staff. The book also delves into creating a compelling brand identity that resonates with customers and explores effective marketing and advertising strategies to attract and retain clients.

Furthermore, this book provides invaluable guidance on pricing your services competitively, managing your finances, and building strong customer relationships. You'll explore strategies for offering additional services and upselling, as well as implementing quality control measures to ensure customer satisfaction. The book also offers practical tips for expanding your business and staying ahead of the competition.

Whether you're a seasoned entrepreneur or a novice in the business world, this book equips you with the knowledge, strategies, and resources to establish a thriving car wash business. Each chapter provides detailed information, actionable steps, and real-world examples to help you navigate the challenges and capitalize on the opportunities in this dynamic industry.

Let's dive in.

Chapter 1:
The Car Wash Business

Before delving into the specifics of launching a car wash business, it's crucial to grasp the essence of the industry and why it presents an enticing entrepreneurial avenue.

The car wash sector has undergone substantial growth lately, propelled by multiple factors. Primarily, the escalating number of vehicles on the roads has sparked a heightened demand for car washing services. In today's bustling pace of life, car owners often grapple with time constraints and lack the expertise needed to preserve their vehicles' visual appeal. This scenario has carved out a specialized market for adept car detailers who can revive and sustain the aesthetic allure of automobiles.

Moreover, many car owners take profound pride in their vehicles, elevating the act of a car wash beyond mere maintenance—it's a mode of self-expression. With a burgeoning emphasis on the aesthetics of vehicles, a meticulously executed car wash can breathe new life into a car, rejuvenating its appearance. The elevated satisfaction levels among customers and the ensuing repeat business render the car wash industry exceptionally lucrative.

As the proprietor of a car wash enterprise, you hold the reins to cater to this demand and furnish car owners with the services required to uphold their vehicles' pristine condition. Your triumph hinges upon your capacity to deliver exemplary outcomes, establish a robust brand, and offer unparalleled customer service.

Why Start a Car Wash Business?

Starting a car wash business offers a multitude of advantages that can make it an appealing entrepreneurial choice. Here are some of the key reasons why you might consider launching your own car wash venture:

Firstly, the car wash industry has shown consistent growth, largely due to the increasing number of vehicles on the roads. With more cars needing regular cleaning and maintenance, there's a perpetual demand for car wash services. This demand provides a stable foundation for a business, offering a consistent flow of customers.

Additionally, the modern lifestyle often leaves car owners with limited time and expertise to clean and maintain their vehicles. This creates a niche market for professional car wash services. As a car wash owner, you can tap into this need, offering convenience and expertise that many car owners seek. A well-executed car wash can go beyond just cleanliness; it's a transformational service. Many car owners take pride in the appearance of their vehicles, considering it a form of self-expression. Providing a thorough and high-quality car wash can not only meet their expectations but also exceed them, resulting in satisfied customers who are likely to become repeat clients.

A car wash business can be relatively scalable. You have the flexibility to offer various services, such as basic washes, detailing, waxing, and more, catering to different customer preferences. With the right marketing strategies and quality service, you can expand your customer base and potentially branch out to multiple locations. Lastly, the overhead costs for a car wash business can be manageable compared to other ventures. While initial setup and equipment investment are necessary, operational costs can be controlled, especially with efficient management practices in place.

In essence, starting a car wash business presents an opportunity to enter a growing industry, cater to a constant demand, provide a valuable service, and potentially build a scalable and profitable enterprise.

While the car wash business offers numerous opportunities, it's important to recognize that success doesn't come without effort, dedication, and a well-thought-out strategy. In the following chapters, we will guide you through the essential steps to start, run, and grow your car wash business. You'll learn about market research and planning, setting up your business, acquiring the necessary skills, branding and marketing, operational strategies, financial management, and much more.

As you read through this guide, remember that every successful car wash business begins with a clear vision, a commitment to excellence, and a customer-centric approach. The road ahead may have its challenges, but with the right knowledge and a strong work ethic, you can navigate them successfully and build a business that not only thrives but also fulfills your passion for cars.

Car wash is more than just cleaning a vehicle's exterior and interior surfaces. It is an art form that requires precision, skill, and a deep understanding of automotive aesthetics. In this chapter, we will delve into the intricacies of car wash and explore the various techniques and processes involved in achieving a flawless finish.

The Basics of Car Wash

Car wash is the process of thoroughly cleaning a vehicle to enhance its appearance. It involves a systematic approach that addresses both the exterior and interior aspects of a car. Whether you're a car enthusiast looking to maintain your vehicle's pristine condition or a professional detailer seeking to expand your knowledge, this chapter will introduce you to the basics of car wash.

Understanding the Importance of Car Wash:
Car wash involves a meticulous process that removes dirt, grime, and contaminants while restoring and protecting various surfaces. Proper car wash not only enhances the aesthetic appeal of a vehicle but also helps preserve its value and extend its lifespan.

Essential Wash Tools and Equipment:
To get started with car wash, you'll need a set of essential tools and equipment. Here are some items you should have in your wash arsenal:

Washing Tools:
To kick things off, you'll want to have a reliable set of washing tools. These are the foundation of any successful wash job.

High-Quality Microfiber Wash Mitts: These mitts are your best friends when it comes to gently and effectively washing the exterior of a car. They are super soft and help minimize the risk of swirl marks or scratches.
Soft Bristle Brushes: Soft brushes come in handy for cleaning wheels, tires, and other hard-to-reach areas. They should be tough on grime but gentle on the finish.
pH-Neutral Car Wash Soap: Opt for a pH-neutral car wash soap to ensure it won't harm the car's paint or wax. It's essential for safely lifting dirt and grime from the surface.

Drying Tools:
Once you've given the car a good wash, it's time to dry it properly to avoid water spots and streaks.

Microfiber Towels: These are your best bet for drying the car. They're super absorbent and won't scratch the paint if used correctly.

Drying Towel Specifically Designed for Automotive Use: These towels are often larger and can absorb a lot of water quickly, making the drying process more efficient.

Polishing and Waxing Tools:
To achieve that glossy, showroom finish, you'll need some specialized tools.

Dual-Action Polisher: A dual-action polisher is a game-changer for removing swirl marks, fine scratches, and enhancing the shine of the paint.
Foam or Microfiber Applicators: These are used to apply polish, wax, or sealant evenly.
Various Polishing Pads: Different pads serve different purposes, from cutting and compounding to finishing and waxing.
Quality Car Wax or Paint Sealant: Choose a high-quality carnauba wax or paint sealant to protect and enhance the vehicle's finish.

Interior Cleaning Tools:
Don't forget about the interior; it's equally important to have a spotless cabin.

Vacuum Cleaner: A powerful vacuum cleaner helps you get rid of dirt, debris, and crumbs from the carpets, seats, and crevices.
Soft Brushes: Use soft brushes to gently clean dust and grime from dashboards, vents, and other interior surfaces.
Microfiber Cloths: Microfiber cloths are your go-to for wiping and polishing interior surfaces without leaving lint or streaks.
Interior-Specific Cleaning Products: You'll need interior cleaners for fabrics, leather, plastics, and glass. These products are specially formulated for each surface to ensure a thorough yet safe clean.

Protective Gear:
Last but not least, ensure your safety and comfort during the wash process.

Gloves: Protect your hands from harsh chemicals, sharp edges, and excessive exposure to water.
Safety Glasses: Shield your eyes from splashes, chemicals, or debris that may be dislodged during cleaning.
Dust Mask: Prevent inhaling dust, fumes, or particles, especially when working on dusty or confined areas.
Having these essential tools and equipment at your disposal sets the stage for successful car wash. Remember, the key to a job well done is not just having the right tools but also knowing how to use them effectively.

Preparing the Vehicle for Wash:
Before you dive into the intricate work of washing a vehicle, you must ensure that the car is in the right condition and the work environment is suitable. Let's break down the steps to prepare your vehicle for wash:

Find a Suitable Location:
Choosing the right location is the first step in the wash process. Here's what you need to consider:

Shaded Area: Select a location that provides shade, especially if you're working on a sunny day. Direct sunlight can cause cleaning agents to dry too quickly, leaving streaks and water spots on the vehicle's surface. A shaded area helps maintain a consistent working environment.

Good Lighting: Adequate lighting is essential for a detailed inspection and to ensure you don't miss any imperfections. Natural daylight or bright artificial lighting is your best friend when it comes to evaluating the vehicle's condition and the quality of your work.

Access to Water: You'll need a water source, whether it's a hose or a pressure washer, for rinsing the vehicle before you start the cleaning process. Make sure your chosen location allows for easy access to water.

Access to Electricity: While not always essential, access to electricity can be convenient for tools like polishers or vacuum cleaners. If you're working in a location without power, ensure your equipment is fully charged or consider using a generator.

Gather Your Tools and Products:
The success of your wash job depends on having the right tools and products at your disposal. Before you begin, make sure you have everything you need:

Checklists: Having a detailed checklist can help you ensure you haven't overlooked any tools or products. It's easy to forget something in the excitement of wash, so a list can be a lifesaver.

Cleaning Agents: Gather all the cleaning agents and wash products you'll need, including car wash soap, degreasers, interior cleaners, wax, and sealants. Having them organized and ready for use will save you time.

Tools: As mentioned in our previous discussion, tools like microfiber wash mitts, soft bristle brushes, polishing pads, and a vacuum cleaner are essential for different aspects of the wash process.

Protective Gear: Don't forget about your safety. Ensure you have gloves, safety glasses, and a dust mask on hand to protect yourself during the wash process.

Remove Personal Belongings:
Now that you have your location and tools ready, it's time to prepare the vehicle itself. Start by removing any personal items from the interior. This includes:

Emptying the Glove Compartment: Remove registration, insurance documents, or any other personal items.

Clearing the Trunk: Ensure the trunk is free from any personal belongings, tools, or spare parts.

Vacating the Center Console: Check between the seats and center console for loose change, pens, or any other small items.

Cleaning Out the Cup Holders: These areas can accumulate dust, crumbs, and even forgotten items.

Removing personal belongings not only ensures a thorough cleaning process but also prevents any potential damage or loss of items during wash.

Rinse and Pre-Wash:
Before you start applying any cleaning agents, it's crucial to rinse the vehicle to remove loose dirt and debris. Follow these steps:

Hose or Pressure Washer: Use a hose or a pressure washer to rinse the vehicle thoroughly. Start from the roof and work your way down, ensuring you cover every surface.

Pre-Wash Solution: After rinsing, apply a pre-wash solution to the vehicle's surface. This solution is designed to break down and soften stubborn grime, making it easier to remove during the wash. Allow the pre-wash solution to dwell for a few minutes, but avoid letting it dry on the car.

Proper preparation sets the stage for a successful wash job, ensuring that you can focus on the artistry of making the vehicle look its best. With the vehicle ready and your tools at hand, you'll be well-equipped to tackle the intricate task of cleaning, polishing, and protecting your car.

Exterior Car Wash:
Before initiating the exterior wash, gather the essential supplies— a hose or pressure washer, two buckets, car wash soap specifically formulated for automobiles, soft microfiber towels or sponges, a soft-bristled brush or mitt, and a drying cloth. Park the vehicle in a shaded area to prevent soap from drying too quickly in the sun, which could lead to water spots.

Start by thoroughly rinsing the vehicle with water. Using a hose or pressure washer, remove loose dirt and debris from all surfaces, including the body panels, windows, wheels, and tires. This initial rinse helps prevent scratching during the subsequent washing process by eliminating larger particles.

Prepare two buckets—one filled with clean water and the other with a proper dilution of car wash soap. Dip the sponge or mitt into the soapy water and begin washing the vehicle, starting from the top and working your way down. Use gentle, circular motions to lift dirt without causing scratches. Periodically rinse the sponge or mitt in the bucket of clean water to prevent dirt from accumulating and potentially scratching the car's surface.

For areas with stubborn dirt or grime, like lower panels and wheels, utilize a separate sponge or soft-bristled brush dedicated to these specific areas. Employ caution and avoid using the same tools used for the body panels to prevent transferring abrasive particles. After thoroughly washing all surfaces, use the hose or pressure washer to rinse off all the soap and suds. Ensure complete removal of soap residue to prevent streaks or water spots from forming during drying.

Once rinsed, use soft, clean microfiber towels to dry the vehicle thoroughly. Pat the surfaces gently rather than rubbing vigorously to avoid potential scratches. Pay special attention to areas prone to water accumulation, such as side mirrors and door handles.

To elevate the exterior finish further, consider applying a coat of wax or sealant for added protection and shine. Additionally, tire cleaning products and specific detailing for chrome or other exterior elements can provide a polished look.

A well-executed exterior car wash not only restores the vehicle's appearance but also safeguards the paint and exterior components from environmental contaminants. Consistent application of these steps ensures a clean, glossy, and well-maintained exterior for your vehicle.

The exterior car wash process is a meticulous art that revolves around rejuvenating the vehicle's exterior surfaces. By focusing on cleaning, restoring, and protecting, detailers can bring out the full glory of a car's paintwork and other exterior features. Here are the key steps involved in this intricate process:

Interior Car Wash:
Interior wash is an essential aspect of the car wash process, focusing on cleansing and reviving the interior surfaces of the

vehicle to provide a clean, comfortable, and aesthetically pleasing environment for both the driver and passengers. The following steps outline a general approach to interior wash:

a. Vacuuming:
The first order of business in interior wash is a thorough vacuuming session. Every nook and cranny of the interior, including seats, carpets, floor mats, and hidden crevices, undergoes meticulous vacuuming. This step ensures the removal of accumulated dust, dirt, and debris, contributing to a fresh and clean interior foundation.

b. Cleaning Surfaces:
With the interior surfaces primed, attention turns to the various components that make up the cabin. Interior-specific cleaners and brushes come into play as detailers work their magic on surfaces such as the dashboard, door panels, center console, and other areas prone to dust and grime buildup. The goal is not only cleanliness but also the restoration of the original luster of these surfaces.

c. Glass and Mirrors:
Clear visibility is paramount for a safe and enjoyable driving experience. Detailers meticulously clean the interior glass and mirrors using a streak-free glass cleaner and a soft, lint-free microfiber cloth. This ensures a crystal-clear view for the driver and passengers, enhancing both safety and the overall aesthetic appeal of the vehicle's interior.

d. Upholstery and Carpet Cleaning:
The upholstery and carpets of a vehicle often bear the brunt of spills, stains, and everyday wear. Detailers address these issues by using suitable cleaners designed specifically for upholstery and carpets. Stubborn stains are treated with care, employing a gentle

scrubbing action to lift and remove the blemishes, leaving the interior looking and feeling rejuvenated.

e. Odor Elimination:
A final touch to the interior wash process involves ensuring that the vehicle not only looks clean but also smells fresh. Detailers use odor eliminators or carefully chosen air fresheners to eliminate any lingering odors and maintain a pleasant scent within the cabin. This step adds the finishing touch to the interior wash experience, creating an inviting atmosphere for anyone entering the vehicle.

Interior wash is more than a cosmetic endeavor; it's about creating a space where the driver and passengers feel comfortable, relaxed, and proud of their vehicle. The attention to detail in cleaning and restoring the interior surfaces reflects not only in the aesthetics but also in the overall in-car experience. As the doors open, the fresh, clean interior becomes a testament to the dedication and expertise of the detailer, leaving a lasting impression on those who step inside.

Car wash is a comprehensive process that requires attention to detail and the use of proper techniques and tools. By understanding the importance of car wash and following the basic steps outlined in this chapter, you'll be well on your way to achieving a professionally detailed vehicle. Remember, practice and patience are key to mastering the art of car wash.

Chapter 2:
Understanding the Car Wash Market

Before diving into the practical aspects of starting a car wash business, it is crucial to gain a deep understanding of the car wash market. In this chapter, we will explore the dynamics of the industry, analyze market trends, identify target customers, and study the competition. To succeed, you need to grasp the ins and outs of this industry.

First and foremost, it's essential to realize that the car wash market is vast and diverse. It caters to a wide range of customers, from everyday drivers who want a clean car to car enthusiasts and collectors who demand meticulous attention to detail. To thrive in this market, you need to define your target audience and tailor your services accordingly.

One key aspect of the car wash market is specialization. You can choose to focus on specific areas, such as paint correction, interior wash, ceramic coating, or even niche markets like luxury cars, classic cars, or off-road vehicles. Understanding what sets you apart and catering to a niche can give your business a competitive edge.

Another critical factor is location. The demand for car wash services can vary depending on where you're situated. Urban areas often have a higher demand, but they also come with more competition. Smaller towns may offer less competition but might have a smaller customer base. Research your local market to assess the demand and competition in your area.

Pricing is a significant consideration. It's essential to offer competitive prices while ensuring you cover your costs and make a profit. Offering different packages and add-on services can help attract a broader range of customers. Keep an eye on your competitors' pricing strategies and adjust yours accordingly.

Building a solid online and social media presence is vital in today's market. Many potential customers search for car wash services online. Utilize websites, social media platforms, and online advertising to reach a broader audience and showcase your work through photos and videos. Positive reviews and testimonials from satisfied customers can also boost your credibility.

Networking within the car wash community and collaborating with local businesses can also be advantageous. Partnering with auto dealerships, car rental companies, or local garages can provide a steady stream of clients.

Finally, never underestimate the importance of customer service. Building a loyal customer base is often based on the trust and satisfaction your clients feel. Always communicate clearly with your customers, manage their expectations, and address any issues promptly.

Market Size and Growth:

Assessing the market size and growth potential is a critical step when starting a car wash business. Understanding the current market conditions and anticipating future trends is essential for making informed decisions and planning for success.

Market Size:
The market size for a car wash business can vary significantly depending on the region, local demand, and economic factors. Typically, larger urban areas tend to have a more extensive market due to the higher population density and the increased number of vehicles. However, even in smaller towns and suburban areas,

there is a consistent demand for car wash services, albeit on a smaller scale.

To determine the market size in your area, consider factors such as the number of registered vehicles, the presence of competitors, and the disposable income of potential customers. Market research, including surveys and data analysis, can help you estimate the potential customer base and the overall market size for your car wash business.

Market Growth:
The car wash industry has been experiencing steady growth over the years for several reasons:

Increasing Vehicle Ownership: As more people own and use vehicles for daily transportation, the need for car wash services continues to grow. With more cars on the road, there is a constant demand for cleaning, maintenance, and restoration.

Consumer Awareness: Customers are becoming more aware of the benefits of regular car wash, not only for aesthetic reasons but also for protecting their investment. This increased awareness has led to a growing interest in professional wash services.

Evolving Vehicle Types: The diversity of vehicles on the road, including luxury cars, sports cars, and electric vehicles, creates opportunities for specialized wash services. Different vehicles have unique needs and requirements, providing a niche market for detailers who can cater to these specific demands.

Online and Mobile Services: The convenience of on-demand and mobile wash services is appealing to many customers. As technology and apps make it easier to book wash services, this segment of the market is expected to continue growing.

While the car wash industry shows promise in terms of market growth, it's essential to be aware of potential challenges. These include increased competition, the need to stay updated with the latest techniques and products, and the necessity of providing excellent customer service to retain and attract clients.

In summary, the market size for a car wash business varies depending on location, but there is a consistent demand for these services across different areas. The market is poised for growth due to increasing vehicle ownership, evolving customer awareness, and the emergence of specialized and eco-friendly services. To succeed in this competitive industry, staying attuned to market trends and adapting your business accordingly is crucial.

Customer Segments:

Understanding the diverse customer segments in the car wash market is crucial for targeting the right audience and tailoring your services to their needs. Here are some key customer segments:

Individual Car Owners: This segment includes car enthusiasts, busy professionals, and individuals who value the appearance and maintenance of their vehicles. They seek professional wash services to keep their cars in top condition.

Fleet Owners and Businesses: Companies with large fleets, car rental agencies, and taxi services are part of this segment. They require regular wash services to maintain their vehicles' aesthetics and protect their investments.

Dealerships and Car Showrooms: Car dealerships and showrooms often offer wash services to enhance the visual appeal of their vehicles and attract potential buyers.

Luxury and Exotic Car Owners: Owners of high-end luxury and exotic vehicles have specific requirements for wash. They seek premium services and specialized treatments to maintain the value and unique features of their cars.

Identifying Your Target Customers

Now, before you plunge into the world of car wash, you've got to know who your dream customers are. Who are they? What makes them tick?

This process involves delving deep into the intricate landscape of potential customers, understanding their nuances, preferences, and needs. Essentially, who are your ideal customers, and what makes them tick?

To undertake this task effectively, a detailed analysis encompassing demographics, psychographics, and behaviors is imperative. Demographics provide the statistical data on age, gender, income, and location, offering a quantitative snapshot of your potential customer base. Psychographics, on the other hand, delve into the qualitative aspects, exploring customers' lifestyles, values, and preferences. Combining these dimensions creates a comprehensive customer profile, a vivid representation of the individuals your business aims to serve.

This customer profile becomes the guiding star for your marketing strategies. Understanding the unique blend of characteristics that define your target market enables you to tailor your services and branding in a way that resonates with them. Whether your focus is on catering to the luxury car owners who seek premium wash services, everyday commuters looking for convenience, or a specific niche with distinct needs, this knowledge becomes the cornerstone of your business strategy.

Knowing your target market is not just about casting a wide net; it's about precision and intentionality. It allows you to craft messaging that speaks directly to the desires and pain points of your ideal customers. It informs the design of your services, ensuring that they align seamlessly with the expectations of the market you aim to capture. In essence, identifying your target market is akin to customizing a key that perfectly fits the lock of your desired customer base.

In the ever-evolving world of car wash, where customer expectations vary widely, this knowledge becomes a powerful tool for differentiation. It sets the stage for effective branding, allowing you to communicate your unique value proposition to the right audience. As you embark on this journey, remember that your target market is not static; it may evolve over time. Regular reassessment and adaptation ensure that your business remains agile and responsive to the dynamic needs of your customers. In the end, the process of identifying your target market is not just a step in starting a business; it's a continuous dialogue with the heart of your enterprise—the customers you serve.

Analyzing Your Competitions

It's crucial to take a close look at the competition. Who are the other players, and what makes each of them unique? By examining their strengths and weaknesses, you uncover opportunities to stand out and bring innovation to your own wash venture. This understanding guides decisions on pricing, services, and customer experience, allowing you to position your business strategically in the competitive landscape.

Start by identifying your fellow competitors—local wash shops, mobile services, or specialists in a specific niche. Then, go beyond mere recognition and dig into what makes each competitor special. Understanding their strengths and weaknesses provides valuable insights that can shape your own business strategy. For example, knowing what services they excel at and where they fall short can help you tailor your offerings to meet customer needs more effectively.

This insight becomes a compass for making strategic decisions in various aspects of your business. Pricing strategies, for instance, can be adjusted based on what competitors charge for similar services. By positioning your pricing competitively while adding extra value, you create an attractive proposition for customers seeking both quality and affordability.

Service offerings can also be refined based on what competitors are doing well or not so well. If a competitor specializes in a specific niche, you might explore alternative niches or enhance your expertise in that area. Similarly, improving the overall customer experience by learning from competitors' successes and addressing their shortcomings is a smart move. Whether it's streamlining booking processes, improving communication, or offering unique perks, this understanding enriches the overall customer journey.

Ultimately, the aim of analyzing the competition is to strategically position your business in the wash landscape. By leveraging insights into your competitors' strengths and weaknesses, you carve out a distinct identity for your venture. This unique identity, grounded in differentiation and innovation, becomes the key to attracting and retaining customers in a competitive market. In the dynamic world of car wash, where every gleam matters, standing out from the competition isn't just a smart move—it's the recipe for long-term success.

Trends and Preferences:

To stay competitive in the car wash market, it's crucial to be aware of emerging trends and customer preferences. Some notable trends include:

Ceramic Coatings: The popularity of ceramic coatings has surged in recent years. These durable coatings provide long-lasting protection to a vehicle's paintwork, reducing the need for frequent waxing.

Eco-Friendly Wash: Environmentally friendly practices, such as using waterless or steam cleaning methods and eco-friendly cleaning products, are gaining traction among environmentally conscious consumers.

Mobile Wash Services: Convenience is a priority for many customers, leading to the rise of mobile wash services. Detailers who offer on-site services, bringing their equipment and expertise directly to the customer, can tap into this growing market segment.

Specialized Wash Services: There is an increasing demand for specialized wash services, such as paint correction, headlight restoration, and interior restoration. These services cater to customers seeking comprehensive restoration or customization for their vehicles.

Business Opportunities:

The car wash business offers a range of business opportunities, and entrepreneurs can explore various avenues to capitalize on this growing industry. Here are some of the business opportunities within the car wash sector:

Mobile Car Wash: Offering mobile car wash services can be a lucrative option. This model involves taking your services directly to customers' locations, whether it's their homes or workplaces. Mobile wash provides convenience for customers who may not have the time or inclination to visit a physical location. It can also be a cost-effective way to start a car wash business since you won't need to invest in a fixed facility.

Specialized Wash Services: There are niche markets within car wash that present opportunities for specialized services. You can focus on specific areas such as paint correction, ceramic coating application, interior wash, or engine bay wash. Specializing in luxury cars, classic cars, or off-road vehicles can also set your business apart and allow you to charge premium rates for your expertise.

Eco-Friendly Wash: With increasing environmental awareness, there is a growing demand for eco-friendly car wash services. Using waterless or low-water methods and environmentally friendly products can attract eco-conscious customers. You can build a business around sustainability and market your services as green and eco-friendly.

Franchise Opportunities: Many successful car wash businesses offer franchise opportunities. Investing in a well-established car wash franchise can provide you with a proven business model, training, and ongoing support. Franchises often come with brand recognition, which can help attract customers more quickly than starting from scratch.

Car Wash Products and Supplies: Running a car wash supply store can be a complementary business. You can sell wash products, equipment, and accessories to both professional detailers and DIY enthusiasts. This business can be conducted online, through a physical store, or a combination of both.

Wash Equipment Rental: Some entrepreneurs have found success in renting out high-end wash equipment to fellow detailers or even car enthusiasts looking to tackle DIY projects. Renting equipment can be a cost-effective way for newcomers to access professional tools.

Subscription Services: Subscription-based car wash services are gaining popularity. Customers can sign up for monthly or quarterly subscriptions, ensuring regular maintenance of their vehicles. Offering these packages can provide a stable and predictable income stream for your business.

Wash Training and Workshops: If you have extensive knowledge and experience in car wash, consider offering training and workshops to aspiring detailers. Sharing your expertise can be a rewarding and profitable venture.

Fleet Wash Services: Partnering with businesses that maintain fleets of vehicles, such as car rental companies, delivery services, or taxi services, can be a consistent source of revenue. Fleet wash services often require regular maintenance and can provide a stable client base.

Online Sales and E-commerce: Operating an e-commerce platform to sell wash products, tools, and accessories can be a lucrative venture. As more customers prefer to shop online, a well-curated online store can attract a wide customer base.

These are just a few of the many business opportunities within the car wash industry. The key is to identify your niche, offer exceptional service, and stay current with industry trends and customer preferences. The car wash market continues to evolve, offering entrepreneurial possibilities for those willing to tap into the demand for quality automotive care.

Understanding the car wash market involves identifying your target audience, specializing in specific areas, considering your location, pricing competitively, building a strong online presence, using top-quality equipment, networking, and providing excellent customer service. By doing your homework and staying dedicated, you can carve a successful niche in the car wash industry.

Chapter 3:
Developing a Business Plan

A well-crafted business plan is the foundation of any successful car wash business. In this chapter, we will guide you through the process of developing a comprehensive business plan that outlines your goals, strategies, financial projections, and operational structure. By taking the time to carefully plan and organize your business, you will have a roadmap to follow and a solid foundation for future growth and success.

Executive Summary:
The executive summary provides an overview of your car wash business plan. It should summarize the key points of your plan, including the business concept, target market, competitive advantage, and financial goals.

Business Description:
In this section, provide a detailed description of your car wash business. Discuss your business structure (sole proprietorship, partnership, LLC, etc.), location, and the services you plan to offer. Explain your unique selling proposition (USP) and how you aim to differentiate your business from competitors.

Market Analysis:
Conduct a thorough market analysis to identify your target market, competitors, and industry trends. Gather data on car ownership rates, demographics, and consumer preferences in your area. Assess the competitive landscape to understand the strengths and weaknesses of existing wash businesses. Identify opportunities for growth and potential challenges you may face.

Services and Pricing:
Outline the wash services you intend to offer and develop a pricing strategy. Consider the cost of materials, labor, overhead expenses, and desired profit margins. Conduct a competitive analysis to ensure your prices are competitive while maintaining profitability. Highlight any unique or specialized services that may set you apart from competitors.

Marketing and Sales Strategy:
Describe your marketing and sales approach to attract customers and generate revenue. Outline your target marketing channels, such as online advertising, social media marketing, partnerships with local businesses, or direct mail campaigns. Consider offering promotional packages, discounts for loyal customers, or referral programs to incentivize customer retention and word-of-mouth referrals.

Operations and Management:
Detail the operational aspects of your car wash business. Describe the equipment, supplies, and facilities required to deliver your services. Outline your staffing needs, including the number of employees, their roles, and any specialized training requirements. Include information about licenses, permits, insurance, and health and safety regulations that apply to your business.

Financial Projections:
Develop a comprehensive financial plan for your car wash business. Include projected revenue, expenses, and cash flow for the first three to five years. Consider factors such as start-up costs, ongoing expenses (rent, utilities, supplies), labor costs, and marketing expenditures. Create financial forecasts based on different scenarios, allowing for contingencies and potential market fluctuations.

Funding and Capitalization:
Determine how you will finance your car wash business. Identify your start-up costs, including equipment purchases, leasehold improvements, marketing expenses, and working capital. Explore financing options such as personal savings, bank loans, or partnerships with investors. Outline your capitalization structure and any potential sources of funding.

Implementation Plan:
Create a timeline and action plan for launching and operating your car wash business. Break down the tasks and milestones, assign responsibilities, and set deadlines. Include key considerations such as securing a location, purchasing equipment, hiring and training staff, and implementing marketing strategies. Review the plan regularly and make adjustments as necessary.

Risk Assessment and Contingency Planning:
Identify potential risks and challenges that may affect your car wash business. Develop contingency plans to mitigate these risks, such as diversifying your customer base, having a financial buffer, or implementing effective quality control measures. Consider external factors like economic downturns, changes in consumer behavior, or increased competition.

Developing a comprehensive business plan is essential for the success of your car wash business. By carefully considering each aspect, from the market analysis to the financial projections, you'll have a roadmap that guides your decision-making and sets the foundation for a thriving business. In the next chapter, we will delve into the legal and regulatory aspects of starting a car wash business, ensuring compliance and protecting your interests.

Chapter 4:
Legal and Regulatory Considerations

Operating a car wash business involves complying with various legal and regulatory requirements. Understanding and adhering to these considerations is essential for running a lawful and compliant business. This chapter will provide an overview of the key legal and regulatory aspects you should be aware of when starting and operating your car wash business.

Business Structure and Registration:
Choose an appropriate business structure for your car wash business, such as a sole proprietorship, partnership, limited liability company (LLC), or corporation. Register your business with the appropriate government authorities, such as obtaining a business license or permit, registering for taxes, and fulfilling any local or state-specific requirements.

Insurance Coverage:
Obtain appropriate insurance coverage to protect your car wash business from potential risks. Consider policies such as general liability insurance, commercial property insurance, workers' compensation insurance (if you have employees), and commercial auto insurance if you have company vehicles. Consult with an insurance professional to assess your specific needs and ensure adequate coverage.

Environmental Regulations:
Car wash involves the use of cleaning agents, chemicals, and wastewater disposal. Familiarize yourself with local, state, and federal environmental regulations regarding the proper handling, storage, and disposal of chemicals and wastewater. Implement environmentally friendly practices, such as using eco-friendly

products, waterless wash methods, and ensuring proper containment and disposal of hazardous materials.

Employment Regulations:
If you plan to hire employees for your car wash business, familiarize yourself with employment regulations and labor laws. Ensure compliance with minimum wage laws, overtime pay, employee classification (e.g., full-time, part-time), payroll taxes, and employment eligibility verification (Form I-9). Establish clear employment policies and procedures, including those related to worker safety, harassment prevention, and discrimination.

Intellectual Property Protection:
Consider protecting your car wash business's intellectual property, such as your business name, logo, and branding materials. Conduct a thorough trademark search to ensure your chosen name or logo does not infringe on existing trademarks. If necessary, consult with an intellectual property attorney to file for trademark registration and protect your brand identity.

Customer Contracts and Liability:
Develop clear and comprehensive customer contracts or service agreements that outline the terms and conditions of your wash services. Include provisions related to pricing, cancellation policies, warranties, limitations of liability, and dispute resolution mechanisms. Consult with a business attorney to ensure your contracts comply with applicable laws and adequately protect your interests.

Privacy and Data Protection:
If you collect and store customer information, such as names, contact details, or payment information, ensure compliance with privacy and data protection laws. Safeguard customer data, implement appropriate security measures, and develop a privacy

policy that outlines how you handle and protect customer information.

Safety and Occupational Health:
Maintain a safe working environment for your employees and customers. Comply with occupational health and safety regulations, including providing necessary safety equipment, training employees on safe handling of chemicals and equipment, and implementing protocols to prevent accidents and injuries.

Local Zoning and Noise Regulations:
Check local zoning regulations to ensure your car wash business is allowed in your chosen location. Some areas may have specific zoning requirements or restrictions on operating certain types of businesses. Additionally, be mindful of noise regulations to avoid disturbances to neighboring businesses or residents.

Contracts with Suppliers and Contractors:
When engaging suppliers or contractors for products, equipment, or services, use written contracts that clearly define the terms, scope of work, delivery schedules, and payment terms. Review contracts carefully, and if needed, consult with an attorney to ensure protection of your interests and minimize potential disputes.

Complying with legal and regulatory requirements is essential for the smooth operation and long-term success of your car wash business. Stay informed about local, state, and federal laws that apply to your business, seek professional guidance when needed, and prioritize ethical practices to maintain compliance and build a strong reputation within the industry.

Chapter 5:
Essential Equipment and Supplies

Equipping your car wash business with the right tools and supplies is crucial for delivering high-quality services and achieving customer satisfaction. In this chapter, we will explore the essential equipment and supplies that every car wash business should have. From cleaning tools and machines to wash products and protective gear, we will cover everything you need to ensure efficient operations and exceptional results.

Cleaning Tools and Equipment
Pressure Washer

A pressure washer is a vital tool for efficiently removing dirt, grime, and stubborn stains from vehicles. Look for a commercial-grade pressure washer with adjustable pressure settings and a range of nozzles to accommodate different surfaces and cleaning requirements.

Vacuum Cleaner

A powerful vacuum cleaner with various attachments is essential for thorough interior cleaning. Opt for a vacuum cleaner specifically designed for automotive use, equipped with upholstery brushes, crevice tools, and a strong suction capacity to effectively remove dirt, debris, and pet hair.

Polisher and Buffer

A dual-action polisher or buffer is indispensable for achieving a smooth and glossy finish on vehicle surfaces. Invest in a high-quality polisher with variable speed settings and interchangeable pads to effectively remove swirl marks, scratches, and oxidation, while enhancing the shine and clarity of the paint.

Wash Products
Car Wash Soap
Choose a high-quality car wash soap that effectively cleans the vehicle's exterior without stripping away wax or sealants. Look for pH-balanced formulas that provide gentle yet thorough cleaning and leave a streak-free finish.

Wash Clay
To remove embedded contaminants from the paint surface, such as tar, industrial fallout, or tree sap, wash clay is used. Select a clay bar or clay mitt that is gentle on the paint and provides sufficient lubrication to prevent marring or scratching.

Polishes and Compounds
Invest in a range of polishes and compounds designed for different stages of paint correction. This includes cutting compounds to remove heavy defects, polishing compounds to refine the finish, and finishing polishes to enhance gloss and clarity.

Wax and Sealants
Waxes and sealants provide a protective layer on the paint surface, enhancing its shine and protecting it from UV rays, contaminants, and environmental elements. Choose from natural waxes or synthetic sealants, considering the durability, ease of application, and longevity of the protection they provide.

Accessories and Protective Gear
Microfiber Towels
Microfiber towels are essential for various wash tasks, including drying, buffing, and applying products. Invest in high-quality microfiber towels that are soft, lint-free, and absorbent to avoid swirl marks or scratches on the paint.

Brushes and Applicators

Have a selection of wash brushes and applicators for reaching tight areas, cleaning intricate parts, and applying products. Look for brushes with soft bristles, specifically designed for different surfaces such as wheels, upholstery, or vents.

Gloves and Protective Clothing

To protect your hands and skin from chemicals and potential hazards, use nitrile gloves and wear suitable protective clothing. Long-sleeved shirts, pants, and closed-toe shoes are recommended to minimize exposure to cleaning agents and ensure personal safety.

Equipping your car wash business with the essential equipment and supplies discussed in this chapter is crucial for delivering exceptional results and maintaining a professional standard of service. Invest in high-quality tools, choose effective wash products, and prioritize the safety of yourself and your employees with proper protective gear. By having the right equipment and supplies, you'll be well-prepared to tackle any wash task and provide a satisfying experience for your customers.

Chapter 6:
Setting Up Your Car Wash Facility

The physical setup of your car wash facility plays a significant role in the efficiency, productivity, and overall success of your business. In this chapter, we will guide you through the process of setting up your car wash facility, from choosing the right business structure to the right location to selecting equipment and creating a safe and functional workspace. By optimizing your facility layout and workflow, you can provide exceptional service to your customers while maximizing your operational capabilities.

Choosing the Right Business Structure

When you're starting your car wash business, the first big decision on your to-do list is figuring out the right business structure. It's a bit like choosing the foundation for your dream house. You've got options: sole proprietorship, partnership, limited liability company (LLC), or corporation. Each choice has its own set of rules when it comes to taxes, who's responsible if things go south, and how the business is managed. This decision isn't just paperwork; it's like drawing the blueprint for the legal and financial side of your business, and it's going to have a big say in where your business goes from here.

Sole Proprietorship:
If you're inclined towards simplicity and full control, a sole proprietorship might be your preference. In this structure, you are the sole operator and decision-maker. However, it's worth noting that this simplicity also means your personal and business finances are intertwined, which could expose you to potential personal liability.

Partnership:

For those who prefer to embark on the entrepreneurial journey with a trusted partner, a partnership structure provides shared responsibility and collaborative decision-making. Similar to sole proprietorships, partnerships don't offer a legal distinction between personal and business assets, impacting liability.

Limited Liability Company (LLC):
The LLC structure strikes a balance by combining elements of sole proprietorships and corporations. It provides personal liability protection for owners (members) while maintaining the flexibility and simplicity of a smaller business. Many small businesses find LLCs appealing due to their favorable tax treatment.

Corporation:
Choosing a corporation establishes a separate legal entity from its owners. This structure provides the highest level of personal liability protection but comes with added complexity and regulatory requirements. Corporations have the ability to issue stock, making them suitable for businesses seeking investment from external sources.

The business structure you choose goes beyond paperwork; it becomes the blueprint that shapes the legal and financial aspects of your wash business. It influences how you report income, the level of personal liability you assume, and the operational flexibility you retain. This decision becomes the groundwork that sets the direction for your venture's growth, governance, and long-term viability.

Choosing the Right Location

When it comes to setting up your car wash business, where you choose to work your wash magic is a big deal. You've got options – you can go for a traditional brick-and-mortar spot or dive into the world of mobile wash. Each choice has its perks and affects things like how easy it is for customers to reach you, your potential client base, and the costs you'll be dealing with. The key here is to create a space that totally vibes with your brand and the experience you want customers to have, because that's what will keep them coming back.

So, think about it. If you go for a brick-and-mortar location, you've got a physical spot where customers can bring their rides for some serious TLC. It's like a home base, giving you a solid local presence and a chance to attract folks passing by.

Now, on the flip side, there's the mobile wash gig. This is where you take the show on the road, bringing your wash skills right to the customer's doorstep. It's all about convenience – appealing to the crowd that wants the service to come to them. You're not tied down to one spot, so you can reach more people in different areas and even hit up events.

Regardless of which route you take, the space you create has to match up with your brand and the kind of experience you want customers to have. Whether it's a cool shop or a mobile setup, the atmosphere matters. A well-designed and customer-friendly space isn't just a backdrop; it's part of the overall experience. And let's face it, a positive vibe goes a long way in making customers stick around and recommend your wash wizardry to their buddies.

So, when you're thinking about your business location, it's not just about the physical spot – it's a strategic move that shapes how your business runs and how customers see you. Whether you're anchoring your wash hub in a brick-and-mortar shop or going mobile, the goal is to create an environment that shouts your brand and makes your customers feel right at home.

For a brick-and-mortar location, the right location is paramount. A visible and easily accessible location, such as near a busy road or shopping center, can help attract walk-in customers. Additionally, ensure that the facility has ample space to accommodate the vehicles you intend to work on simultaneously. Adequate space allows you to move around vehicles comfortably and store equipment and supplies efficiently. Here are some other factors to consider when choosing the best location:

Zoning and Regulations: Be aware of local zoning regulations and business licenses required for your facility. These regulations can vary by location, so it's essential to check with your local government or municipality to ensure compliance.

Facility Layout: Consider the layout of your facility. An efficient design can improve workflow and productivity. Separate areas for washing, interior wash, paint correction, and product storage can help streamline your operations. Proper ventilation and lighting are also crucial to create a comfortable and safe working environment.

Utilities and Infrastructure: Ensure that your facility has access to necessary utilities like water, electricity, and drainage. These are vital for washing, operating equipment, and maintaining a clean workspace. Depending on your location, you might need to invest in water reclamation systems to comply with environmental regulations.

Storage and Inventory: Organize your facility to include dedicated storage areas for wash products and supplies. Maintain an organized inventory system to track the usage of chemicals, towels, and other consumables to prevent unnecessary wastage and restock items promptly.

Safety and Compliance: Ensure that your facility complies with safety standards. Implement safety measures such as fire extinguishers, first aid kits, and safety signage. Training your employees on safe practices is also essential to prevent accidents and ensure compliance with occupational health and safety regulations.

Aesthetic Considerations: Your facility's appearance can make a significant impression on customers. A clean, well-maintained facility can instill confidence in your services. Consider branding and signage to make your facility easily recognizable and appealing to potential customers.

Employee Amenities: If you plan to hire employees, provide them with appropriate amenities. Break rooms, restrooms, and comfortable workspaces can improve employee morale and productivity.

Environmental Considerations: Car wash often involves the use of chemicals, so it's crucial to implement eco-friendly practices. Invest in equipment and products that minimize water usage and reduce environmental impact. This can also be a selling point for environmentally conscious customers.

Security: Implement security measures to protect your facility and the vehicles you're working on. Surveillance cameras, alarms, and secure access can deter theft and vandalism.

Setting up your car wash facility requires careful planning and attention to detail. A well-organized and efficient workspace can help you provide top-notch services, ensure customer satisfaction, and create a strong foundation for your car wash business to thrive.

Facility Design and Layout:

Designing your car wash facility is a critical aspect of establishing an efficient and customer-friendly business. A well-thought-out facility layout not only enhances workflow efficiency but also contributes to a professional and pleasant working environment. To create an optimal facility, consider the following elements:

Reception Area:
The reception area is the first point of contact for your customers and plays a crucial role in making a positive first impression. Design it to be welcoming, professional, and customer-oriented. Here are some key considerations:

Reception Desk: Install a well-designed reception desk where customers can check in, make appointments, and inquire about services. Equip it with essential office supplies, such as appointment books and payment processing equipment.

Comfortable Seating: Provide comfortable seating for customers who may need to wait while their vehicle is being detailed. Ensure the seating area is well-lit and decorated with your branding or automotive-themed decor.

Service Menu: Display a service menu on the wall or at the reception desk. Clearly list the available services, their prices, and any special offers. This information can help customers make informed decisions.

Customer Information Area: Set up a space where customers can fill out or update their contact information, preferences, and vehicle details. This area should have all the necessary forms and a comfortable workstation with seating.

Wash Bays:
The wash bays are where the magic happens. Allocating sufficient space for wash bays is essential to ensure that vehicles can be serviced with precision and efficiency. Consider the following when planning your wash bays:

Ample Space: Each wash bay should be spacious enough to comfortably accommodate the vehicle being serviced and allow detailers to move around it with ease. Adequate space ensures precision in wash work.

Optimal Lighting: Install excellent lighting in each bay to ensure that detailers can see every detail and flaw on the vehicle's surface. A combination of natural and artificial light can be beneficial.

Ventilation and Climate Control: Proper ventilation is vital to remove fumes and maintain air quality. In regions with extreme temperatures, heating and cooling systems may be necessary to provide a comfortable working environment for detailers.

Utility Connections: Ensure that wash bays have access to electricity, compressed air, and other utilities required for various wash tasks. Convenient utility connections save time and effort.

Washing and Cleaning Area:
The washing and cleaning area is where vehicles are prepared for wash. It's crucial to designate a separate area for this purpose, complete with proper drainage systems and water supply. Consider the following when planning this section:

Water Supply and Drainage: Ensure an ample water supply for washing and cleaning activities. Implement an effective drainage system to prevent standing water and facilitate environmentally friendly waste disposal.

Pressure Washers and Steam Cleaners: Equip this area with high-quality pressure washers and steam cleaners to efficiently remove dirt and grime from vehicles' exteriors. Properly organize and store these tools for easy access.

Cleaning Agents: Allocate storage space for cleaning agents, soaps, shampoos, and other wash-related products. Organize them efficiently to minimize clutter and enhance work efficiency.

Product and Equipment Storage:
Efficient organization and storage of wash products, cleaning agents, equipment, and tools are essential for a smooth workflow. Here's what to consider when planning this area:

Shelving and Cabinets: Install sturdy shelves and cabinets to store wash products and supplies. Categorize items and label shelves to facilitate quick and easy access.

Tool Organization: Develop a system for organizing wash tools, such as brushes, microfiber towels, and buffing pads. Wall-mounted tool racks or pegboards can help keep tools within reach.

Inventory Management: Implement an inventory management system to track product usage and restocking needs. Regularly assess your inventory to ensure you have an adequate supply of essential products.

Employee Facilities:
To create a comfortable and motivating work environment for your employees, provide the following amenities:

Break Area: Dedicate a comfortable break area where employees can relax during their breaks. Furnish it with seating, tables, and amenities like a refrigerator, microwave, and coffee maker.

Restroom Facilities: Ensure that your facility has clean and well-maintained restroom facilities for both employees and customers. Regular cleaning and stocking of supplies are essential.

Personal Belongings Storage: Provide secure storage for employees' personal belongings, such as lockers or designated areas. This helps keep the workspace organized and ensures employees' belongings are safe.

Designing your car wash facility to optimize workflow efficiency and create a pleasant working environment is a crucial step in the success of your business. A well-organized reception area, spacious wash bays, a dedicated washing and cleaning area, efficient product and equipment storage, and employee amenities contribute to the overall professionalism and functionality of your facility. Taking the time to carefully plan and design your facility ensures that your car wash business can operate smoothly and provide top-notch services to your customers.

Chapter 7:
Hiring and Managing Employees

As your car wash business grows, you may need to hire and manage a team of employees to meet customer demand and expand your operations. This chapter will guide you through the process of hiring and effectively managing employees, ensuring a productive and positive work environment.

Defining Roles and Responsibilities

Before hiring employees, clearly define the roles and responsibilities within your car wash business. Determine the specific tasks and duties required for each position, such as wash technicians, customer service representatives, or administrative staff. This will help you identify the necessary skills and qualifications when recruiting. Each member of your team has a crucial part to play, contributing to the overall success of your venture. Let's break down how you can define roles and responsibilities to ensure top-notch wash excellence:

1. Wash Technicians:
At the core of your operation are the wash technicians—the artists who bring vehicles to a state of pristine beauty. Their job includes washing, polishing, waxing, and restoring both the exterior and interior of vehicles. These folks need specialized skills in paint correction, upholstery care, and an eagle eye for detail.

2. Customer Service Representatives:
The frontline faces of your business, customer service representatives interact directly with clients. Their gig involves scheduling appointments, dealing with customer inquiries, and making sure everyone walks away with a positive customer experience. Being friendly and having great communication skills are a must for this role.

3. Operations Manager:

The conductor of the wash symphony, the operations manager oversees the day-to-day workings of the business. This role involves coordinating schedules, managing resources, and making sure everything runs like a well-oiled machine. Strong organizational and leadership skills are key to keeping things smooth.

4. Marketing and Outreach Specialist:

Driving visibility and attracting customers fall under the marketing and outreach specialist's domain. They're responsible for developing marketing strategies, managing the social media game, and implementing cool promotional campaigns. Being creative and having a finger on the pulse of market trends are big assets in this role.

5. Quality Control Inspector:

To keep the quality of your wash services sky-high, a quality control inspector is a must. This job involves doing thorough inspections of completed work, making sure it meets the high standards you've set. Attention to detail and a commitment to excellence are the hallmarks of this crucial position.

6. Administrative Support:

Behind the scenes, administrative support staff handle tasks like bookkeeping, scheduling, and keeping the office shipshape. Their work contributes to the smooth administrative functioning of the business, freeing up other team members to focus on their specialized roles.

7. Business Owner/Manager:

As the visionary leader, the business owner or manager sets the overall direction and strategy for the wash business. Their responsibilities include decision-making, keeping an eye on the finances, and planning for the long term. Leadership skills and a deep understanding of the wash industry are crucial in this pivotal role.

Defining these roles and responsibilities creates a harmonious team, where each member brings their unique skills to the table. Clear communication, ongoing training, and a shared commitment to excellence form the foundation for a team that not only meets but surpasses customer expectations, leaving a lasting shine on every vehicle that rolls through your wash haven.

Recruitment and Selection:
Once you have defined the needed roles, the next step is to recruit. Develop an effective recruitment strategy to attract qualified candidates. Consider various methods, including online job postings, social media platforms, industry-specific job boards, and local advertising. Review resumes, conduct interviews, and assess candidates based on their skills, experience, and cultural fit. Consider background checks and reference checks to verify qualifications and ensure a reliable workforce.

Training and Onboarding

Staying at the forefront of industry advancements is key to delivering top-notch services. Providing ongoing training on new techniques and products is not just a practice; it's a commitment to excellence. Regular training sessions empower wash technicians with the latest skills and insights, ensuring they are well-equipped to handle evolving customer demands. Whether it's incorporating cutting-edge polishing techniques, mastering innovative paint protection methods, or staying abreast of eco-friendly wash products, continuous training elevates the expertise of your team.

These sessions serve as a knowledge exchange platform, fostering a culture of learning and adaptability within the wash business. As the automotive wash landscape evolves, so do customer expectations. Ongoing training allows your team to meet and exceed these expectations, offering services that not only meet industry standards but also showcase a commitment to staying ahead of the curve.

Moreover, keeping your team updated on the latest products ensures they are well-versed in using environmentally friendly and technologically advanced wash solutions. This not only aligns with the growing demand for sustainable practices but also positions your business as a forward-thinking player in the competitive wash market.

In the end, providing ongoing training isn't just an investment in skills; it's an investment in the reputation and success of your car wash business. It creates a team that is not only adept at current practices but also ready to embrace the innovations that shape the future of the industry. As the wash landscape continues to evolve, a well-trained team becomes a driving force, ensuring that your business not only keeps up but stands out in delivering exceptional and cutting-edge wash services.

Creating a positive work environment

Creating a positive work environment in a car wash business is instrumental in fostering a culture of collaboration, enthusiasm, and excellence. It goes beyond the wash bays and administrative offices; it's about cultivating a space where every team member feels valued and motivated. Open communication is a cornerstone of a positive work environment. Encouraging team members to voice their ideas, concerns, and suggestions creates a sense of belonging and contributes to a collaborative atmosphere.

Recognition and appreciation play a pivotal role in shaping a positive workplace. Acknowledging the hard work and dedication of wash technicians, customer service representatives, and support staff fosters a culture of gratitude. Regular praise and recognition not only boost morale but also inspire a sense of pride in one's work.

Providing opportunities for professional growth is another key element. Offering training programs, skill development sessions, and avenues for career advancement demonstrates a commitment to the personal and professional well-being of the team. This investment not only enhances the skills of individual team members but also contributes to the overall expertise and efficiency of the business.

The physical workspace also plays a role in creating a positive environment. A clean, organized, and well-equipped wash facility enhances the overall work experience. It reflects a commitment to professionalism and sets the stage for a conducive and inspiring atmosphere.

Balancing work demands with a supportive work-life balance is crucial. Implementing flexible scheduling, providing breaks, and fostering a sense of camaraderie contribute to a healthy and positive work environment. When team members feel supported both professionally and personally, it translates into increased job satisfaction and a more harmonious workplace.

In essence, creating a positive work environment in a car wash business is about investing in the well-being and growth of your team. It's about building a culture where collaboration is celebrated, accomplishments are recognized, and each team member is motivated to contribute their best. A positive work environment not only enhances employee satisfaction but also radiates through the services provided, contributing to a customer experience that reflects the passion and positivity within the wash team.

Chapter 8:
Marketing and Promoting Your Car Wash Business

Effective marketing and promotion are essential for attracting customers and establishing a strong presence in the competitive car wash industry. In this chapter, we will explore various marketing strategies and techniques that will help you reach your target audience, build brand awareness, and generate consistent business. By implementing a well-rounded marketing plan, you can effectively showcase your services and differentiate yourself from competitors.

Branding and Identity

Building a strong brand identity is a crucial foundation for your car wash business. In this section, you'll learn about the key elements of branding and how to create a compelling brand identity. Define your brand values, mission statement, and unique selling proposition (USP). Develop a memorable brand name, logo, and visual identity that resonate with your target market. Consistently apply your brand across all marketing materials and customer touchpoints to build recognition and trust.

Brand Positioning
Identify your target market and establish your brand positioning. Determine the specific customer segments you want to target, such as luxury car owners, local car enthusiasts, or commercial fleet operators. Differentiate your car wash business by highlighting your unique value proposition, whether it's exceptional customer service, eco-friendly practices, or specialized wash techniques.

Visual Identity
Create a visually appealing and cohesive brand identity that reflects your business values and appeals to your target audience. Design a

professional logo, select a consistent color palette, and choose fonts that align with your brand personality. Use these elements consistently across your website, social media profiles, printed materials, and signage to create a cohesive and recognizable brand presence.

Online Presence and Digital Marketing

In today's digital age, having a strong online presence is vital for reaching and engaging with potential customers. In this section, we will explore various digital marketing strategies and tools to promote your car wash business.

Website Development

Develop a professional website that serves as the online hub for your car wash business. Optimize it for search engines by incorporating relevant keywords and providing informative and engaging content. Include essential information such as your services, pricing, contact details, and customer testimonials. Ensure your website is mobile-friendly and easy to navigate to provide a positive user experience.

Search Engine Optimization (SEO)

Execute SEO strategies to improve your website's visibility. Conduct keyword research to identify the terms your potential customers are using to search for car wash services. Optimize your website's content headings and meta tags to align with these keywords. Build backlinks from reputable websites to enhance your website's authority and search engine rankings.

Social Media Marketing

Utilize social media platforms to connect with your target audience and build brand awareness. Create profiles on platforms such as Facebook, Instagram, and Twitter, and regularly post engaging content related to car wash, industry tips, before-and-after photos, and customer testimonials. Interact with your followers, respond to comments and inquiries promptly, and leverage social media advertising to reach a wider audience.

Online Advertising

Consider running online advertising campaigns to increase your visibility and drive traffic to your website. Platforms such as Google Ads and social media advertising allow you to target specific demographics and locations. Create compelling ad copies and utilize eye-catching visuals to capture the attention of potential customers. Monitor and analyze the performance of your ads, so you can optimize your campaigns for better results.

Traditional Marketing Methods

While digital marketing is essential, traditional marketing methods can still be effective in reaching a local audience. In this section, we will explore traditional marketing strategies that can complement your online efforts.

Print Advertising

Place print advertisements in local newspapers, magazines, and community publications to target a local audience. Design visually appealing ads that highlight your unique selling points and include your contact information and website. Consider distributing flyers or brochures in strategic locations such as car dealerships, auto repair shops, and local events.

Direct Mail Marketing

Reach potential customers directly through targeted direct mail campaigns. Create compelling mailers that showcase your services, special promotions, or exclusive discounts. Develop a mailing list based on demographics and location to ensure you reach the most relevant audience. Personalize your mailers to make a lasting impression and encourage recipients to take action.

Local Partnerships and Referral Programs

Build relationships with other local businesses that complement your car wash services. Collaborate with auto dealerships, car rental companies, or auto body shops to offer referral programs or cross-promotions. Provide incentives for referrals, such as discounts or free add-on services. Word-of-mouth recommendations can be powerful in generating new customers.

Customer Relationship Management (CRM)

Maintaining strong relationships with your customers is crucial for repeat business and positive word-of-mouth. In this section, we will explore customer relationship management strategies to enhance customer satisfaction and loyalty.

Exceptional Customer Service

Deliver exceptional customer service at every touchpoint. Train your employees to be knowledgeable about the business, friendly, and attentive to customer needs. Provide personalized recommendations and go the extra mile to exceed expectations. Encourage customer feedback and promptly address any concerns or issues to ensure a positive experience.

Loyalty Programs

Start a loyalty program to reward repeat customers. This willi improve customer retention. Offer incentives such as discounted services, loyalty points, or exclusive promotions for loyal customers. Maintain a customer database to track and reward customer loyalty.

Customer Reviews and Testimonials
Encourage satisfied customers to leave positive reviews and testimonials online. Display these reviews on your website and social media profiles to build trust and credibility. Respond to both positive and negative reviews in a professional and timely manner to show that you value customer feedback.

Implementing a comprehensive marketing plan will help you promote your car wash business effectively and reach your target audience. By establishing a strong brand identity, optimizing your online presence, utilizing traditional marketing methods, and prioritizing customer relationship management, you can attract new customers, build a loyal customer base, and position your business for long-term success. In the next chapter, we will delve into the operational aspects of running a car wash business, including scheduling, pricing, and quality control.

Chapter 9:
Financial Management for Car Wash Businesses

Proper financial management is crucial for the success and growth of your car wash business. In this chapter, we will discuss key financial management strategies and best practices to help you maintain financial stability, track your business's performance, and make informed decisions for future growth.

Budgeting and Financial Planning

Creating a comprehensive budget and financial plan is crucial for effective financial management in your car wash business. Let's delve into strategies for budgeting and financial planning to ensure the fiscal health of your enterprise.

Revenue Forecasting
Begin by developing a robust revenue forecasting model. Utilize historical data, analyze market trends, and factor in anticipated growth to estimate your expected income for each month or quarter. Consider elements like seasonal fluctuations, the impact of marketing campaigns, and the introduction of new services. This forecasting model establishes a baseline for your budgeting and financial planning endeavors.

Expense Management
For a clear understanding of your financial landscape, meticulously track and categorize your business expenses. Identify areas where costs can be reduced or spending optimized without compromising service quality. This may involve negotiating favorable deals with suppliers, streamlining operational processes, or implementing cost-saving measures. A detailed expense management approach ensures a judicious allocation of resources.

Cash Flow Management

Maintaining a healthy cash flow is vital for the day-to-day operations of your car wash business. Keep a close eye on your cash flow, ensuring sufficient working capital to cover expenses and seize growth opportunities. Implement effective strategies such as prompt invoicing, encouraging early payments, and establishing clear payment terms with customers. These measures contribute to the stability and liquidity necessary for sustained business operations.

A well-crafted budget and financial plan serve as the financial compass for your car wash business. By forecasting revenue, managing expenses judiciously, and optimizing cash flow, you lay the groundwork for financial stability and resilience. These practices not only ensure the smooth functioning of your operations but also position your business to thrive in the dynamic and competitive landscape of the car wash industry.

Financial Analysis and Reporting

Regular financial analysis and reporting provide valuable insights into the financial health and performance of your car wash business. In this section, we will discuss strategies for financial analysis and reporting.

Key Performance Indicators (KPIs)

Identify and track key performance indicators that are relevant to your car wash business. These may include metrics such as revenue per customer, average ticket size, customer acquisition cost, and profit margins. Analyze these KPIs regularly to assess your business's performance, identify areas for improvement, and make data-driven decisions.

Financial Statements

Prepare accurate and up-to-date financial statements, including income statements, balance sheets, and cash flow statements. These statements provide a comprehensive overview of your business's financial position and performance. Regularly review these statements to monitor profitability, identify trends, and evaluate your business's financial stability.

Financial Ratios

Calculate and analyze financial ratios that provide insights into your car wash business's financial health and efficiency. These ratios may include liquidity ratios, profitability ratios, and efficiency ratios. Comparing these ratios to industry benchmarks or historical data can help you assess your business's performance and identify areas that require attention.

Capital Investment and Financing

As your car wash business grows, you may need to consider capital investment and financing options to support expansion efforts. In this section, we will explore strategies for capital investment and financing.

Capital Expenditures

Identify areas where capital investments can improve the efficiency or quality of your car wash operations. This may include purchasing advanced equipment, upgrading your facility, or investing in technology solutions. Conduct a cost-benefit analysis to evaluate the potential return on investment and make informed decisions about capital expenditures.

Financing Options

Explore financing options such as business loans, lines of credit, or equipment leasing to secure the necessary funds for growth initiatives. Research different lenders and financing institutions to find the most favorable terms and interest rates. Prepare a comprehensive business plan and financial projections to present to lenders and increase your chances of securing financing.

Effective financial management is essential for the long-term success and growth of your car wash business. By implementing strategies for budgeting and financial planning, conducting regular financial analysis and reporting, and exploring capital investment and financing options, you can ensure the financial stability and prosperity of your business.

Chapter 10:
Operations and Quality Control in Car Wash

Efficient operations and quality control are vital to ensure the smooth functioning of your car wash business and deliver exceptional service to your customers. In this chapter, we will delve into the operational aspects of running a car wash business, including scheduling, pricing strategies, workflow management, and implementing quality control measures. By establishing effective processes and maintaining high standards, you can optimize productivity, customer satisfaction, and overall business success.

Scheduling and Appointment Management

Effectively managing your schedule and appointments is crucial for maintaining a steady workflow and meeting customer expectations. In this section, we will explore strategies and tools to streamline your scheduling process.

Online Booking System
Implement an online booking system that allows customers to schedule appointments conveniently. Utilize a user-friendly platform that displays available time slots, allows for service customization, and sends automated reminders to customers. This not only improves customer satisfaction but also optimizes your scheduling process by reducing the need for manual appointment coordination.

Efficient Time Management
Develop an efficient time management system to maximize productivity and minimize downtime. Allocate realistic time slots for each service based on the complexity and scope of the wash job. Consider factors such as vehicle size, service package, and any

additional requests from the customer. Optimize your schedule by grouping similar services together and allowing sufficient time for thorough cleaning and drying.

Pricing Strategies

Establishing the right pricing structure is essential for profitability and competitiveness in the car wash industry. In this section, we will explore different pricing strategies and considerations.

Cost Analysis

Conduct a thorough cost analysis to determine the expenses associated with your car wash services. Consider factors such as labor costs, overhead expenses, materials, and equipment maintenance. Factor in a desired profit margin while ensuring your pricing remains competitive within the local market.

Value-Based Pricing

Consider implementing a value-based pricing strategy that reflects the quality of your services and the unique value you provide to customers. Highlight the benefits of your wash techniques, use of high-quality products, and exceptional customer service. Communicate the value proposition effectively to justify your pricing to customers.

Workflow Management

Efficient workflow management ensures smooth operations and consistent service delivery. In this section, we will discuss strategies to optimize your workflow and increase efficiency.

Standard Operating Procedures

Develop comprehensive standard operating procedures (SOPs) for each wash service you offer. Clearly define the steps, techniques, and quality standards for various wash tasks. Train your employees on these SOPs to ensure consistency in service delivery and minimize errors.

Workflow Analysis
Analyze your workflow to identify bottlenecks, inefficiencies, and opportunities for improvement. Evaluate the sequence of tasks, employee responsibilities, and equipment utilization. Streamline the workflow by rearranging tasks, eliminating redundancies, and utilizing automation or specialized tools where appropriate.

Quality Control Measures
Maintaining high-quality standards is essential for customer satisfaction and your business reputation. In this section, we will explore quality control measures to ensure consistent service excellence.

Inspections and Checklists
Implement a rigorous inspection process to review completed wash work. Develop detailed checklists that outline the specific areas and tasks to be inspected for each service. Assign trained inspectors or supervisors to conduct thorough inspections and address any deficiencies promptly.

Customer Feedback and Satisfaction Surveys
Encourage customer feedback through satisfaction surveys or follow-up calls. Regularly assess customer satisfaction to identify areas for improvement. Use feedback to address any service gaps, enhance customer experience, and make necessary adjustments to maintain high-quality standards.

Efficient operations and quality control are essential for the success of your car wash business. By effectively managing scheduling, implementing appropriate pricing strategies, optimizing workflow, and maintaining stringent quality control measures, you can provide exceptional service to your customers while maximizing productivity and profitability. In the next chapter, we will explore strategies for customer retention and building long-term relationships in the car wash industry.

Chapter 11:
Customer Retention and Building Long-Term Relationships

In the competitive car wash industry, building strong relationships with your customers is key to long-term success. In this chapter, we will discuss strategies for customer retention and cultivating loyal, repeat clientele. By focusing on customer satisfaction, effective communication, and providing added value, you can foster trust, loyalty, and positive word-of-mouth recommendations.

Exceptional Customer Service

Exceptional customer service is the heartbeat of success for any car wash business. It goes beyond just giving a car a shiny finish; it's about creating an experience that customers won't forget.

Understanding your customers is the first step. Take the time to listen to their needs, preferences, and any specific requests they might have about the wash process. This personal touch builds trust and sets the stage for a positive customer experience.

Communication is crucial. Keep your customers in the loop about the wash process, timelines, and any extra services you might recommend. Being transparent builds confidence and ensures that customers are well-informed, avoiding surprises and potential misunderstandings.

Just as you pay close attention to every detail of a vehicle during wash, the same level of attention should extend to customer interactions. Respond promptly to inquiries, address concerns with care, and show a dedication to excellence in every aspect of your service.

Exceptional customer service often means going above and beyond. Whether it's offering a complimentary service, sharing useful maintenance tips, or simply making sure the customer feels valued, these extra efforts contribute to a memorable and positive experience.

In the rare instance of an issue, how it's resolved matters. Handle concerns professionally, empathetically, and with a focus on finding solutions. Quick and effective resolution not only addresses the immediate problem but also demonstrates your commitment to customer satisfaction.

Actively seek feedback from your customers. Whether through surveys, reviews, or direct conversations, understanding their thoughts and experiences helps you continually refine and improve your customer service. Feedback is a valuable tool for enhancing the overall customer journey.

Exceptional customer service isn't just about one-time transactions; it's about building lasting relationships. Cultivate a customer-centric approach that values long-term connections. Building a base of satisfied and loyal customers not only ensures repeat business but also establishes your wash business as a trusted and preferred choice in the competitive market.

In essence, exceptional customer service in the car wash industry is a holistic commitment to customer satisfaction. By understanding, communicating effectively, paying attention to details, going the extra mile, resolving issues promptly, soliciting feedback, and building lasting relationships, you not only meet but exceed customer expectations. This dedication not only sets your business apart but also transforms satisfied customers into enthusiastic advocates for your wash services.

Customer Loyalty Programs

Implementing customer loyalty programs can incentivize repeat business and cultivate customer loyalty. In this section, we will explore different loyalty program strategies to reward and retain your valuable customers.

Point-Based Systems

Create a point-based loyalty system where customers earn points for every car wash service they receive. Accumulated points can be redeemed for discounts, free add-on services, or exclusive perks. Ensure the program is easy to understand, track, and redeem points.

VIP Memberships

Offer exclusive VIP memberships to your loyal customers. VIP members can enjoy special privileges such as priority scheduling, discounted rates, exclusive promotions, or access to premium services. Promote the benefits of VIP membership to encourage customers to join and remain loyal to your business.

Customer Feedback and Follow-Up

Proactively seeking customer feedback and conducting follow-up actions demonstrate your commitment to continuous improvement and customer satisfaction. In this section, we will explore effective strategies for gathering feedback and utilizing it to enhance your services.

Satisfaction Surveys

Send satisfaction surveys to your customers after their car wash service. Use these surveys to gather feedback on their experience, gauge satisfaction levels, and identify areas for improvement.

Ensure the surveys are concise, easy to complete, and offer an incentive for participation.

Addressing Customer Concerns

Promptly address any customer concerns or issues that arise. Implement a system for tracking and resolving customer complaints and feedback. Respond to customer inquiries and complaints with empathy, professionalism, and a genuine desire to rectify the situation. Resolve issues promptly and offer appropriate solutions or compensation when necessary.

Added Value Services and Special Promotions

Providing added value services and special promotions can entice customers to return and create a sense of exclusivity. In this section, we will explore strategies for offering added value and promotions.

Add-On Services

Identify additional services that complement your car wash offerings and provide added value to customers. Offer services such as paint protection, upholstery cleaning, or headlight restoration. Recommend these services based on individual customer needs and vehicle condition, enhancing their overall experience.

Seasonal Promotions and Packages

Create seasonal promotions or packages that align with customer needs and preferences. Offer special discounts or bundled services during specific times of the year or in conjunction with holidays or events. Promote these promotions through various marketing channels to attract new and returning customers.

By prioritizing exceptional customer service, implementing customer loyalty programs, actively seeking feedback, and providing added value, you can retain customers and build long-term relationships in the car wash industry. Creating a positive customer experience and fostering loyalty will not only increase customer retention but also generate positive word-of-mouth recommendations, ultimately contributing to the growth and success of your business. In the next chapter, we will explore strategies for expanding your car wash business and reaching new markets.

Chapter 12:
Expanding Your Car Wash Business

Expanding your car wash business can lead to increased revenue, broader market reach, and new opportunities. In this chapter, we will explore strategies and considerations for expanding your operations, attracting new customers, and entering new markets. By carefully planning and implementing growth initiatives, you can take your car wash business to the next level.

Market Research and Analysis

Before considering expansion, it is crucial to conduct thorough market research and analysis to pinpoint potential growth opportunities. This involves delving into market demand, competition, and customer preferences. Let's explore strategies for this vital examination.

Begin by segmenting your target market based on factors such as demographics, psychographics, and geographic location. Identify specific customer segments that align with your services and tailor your marketing efforts accordingly. This understanding of your target market enables the development of effective marketing messages and strategies that resonate with the needs and preferences of your audience.

Conducting a comprehensive analysis of your competitors is essential. Gain insights into their strengths, weaknesses, and market positioning. Evaluate elements like pricing, service offerings, marketing strategies, and customer satisfaction levels. Armed with this information, you can carve out a distinct identity for your car wash business, utilizing unique selling propositions to set yourself apart in the market.

Ways to Expand Your Business

Here are different options to considered in expanding your car wash business:

Geographic Expansion

Expanding geographically allows you to tap into new customer bases and increase your market share. To initiate this expansion, the first step is identifying potential target locations. This involves a careful consideration of factors such as population density, the local demand for car wash services, and the existing competition in each area. A thorough analysis of demographic data, economic indicators, and the overall business environment in potential locations is crucial to assess their viability for your business.

The selection of target locations should align closely with your identified target market and offer substantial growth potential. Understanding the unique characteristics and preferences of the local population will enable you to tailor your services to meet their specific needs, enhancing the chances of successful integration into the new geographical areas.

In essence, strategic geographical expansion involves a meticulous evaluation of potential locations, ensuring they align with your business objectives and hold promise for capturing untapped markets. This thoughtful approach sets the stage for a successful expansion, allowing your car wash business to not only meet but exceed the expectations of new customers in diverse locations.

Franchising or Licensing

Consider franchising or licensing your car wash business as a way to expand rapidly. This allows you to leverage the resources and expertise of franchisees or licensees while maintaining control over brand standards and quality. Develop a comprehensive franchise or licensing program that outlines expectations, training, and ongoing support for partners.

Diversification of Services
Diversifying your service offerings can attract new customers and increase revenue streams. In this section, we will discuss strategies for expanding your car wash services.

Specialized Services
Identify specialized services that align with customer needs and differentiate your business from competitors. Offer services such as ceramic coating, paint correction, or interior restoration. Invest in the necessary training, equipment, and products to deliver high-quality specialized services.

Mobile Wash
Consider offering mobile wash services to cater to customers who prefer the convenience of having their vehicles detailed at their location. Invest in a well-equipped mobile unit and develop efficient scheduling and logistics systems. Market your mobile services to businesses, residential areas, and events to maximize your reach.

Strategic Partnerships and Collaborations
Forming strategic partnerships and collaborations can expand your customer base and increase brand visibility. In this section, we will explore partnership opportunities for your car wash business.

Auto Dealerships and Rental Companies
Collaborate with local auto dealerships and rental companies to offer discounted wash services to their customers. Establish mutually beneficial partnerships where you can benefit from their

customer base and they can enhance their vehicle sales or rental experience.

Corporate Partnerships
Form partnerships with corporate clients to provide ongoing wash services for their fleet vehicles. This can include businesses with company-owned vehicles, car rental agencies, or transportation companies. Develop customized packages and pricing structures to meet their specific needs and offer convenience.

Expanding your car wash business requires careful planning, market analysis, and strategic decision-making. By conducting thorough market research, exploring geographic expansion opportunities, diversifying your service offerings, and forming strategic partnerships, you can position your business for growth and success. In the next chapter, we will discuss strategies for effectively managing your expanding car wash operations.

Conclusion

Starting a car wash business can be a rewarding and profitable venture if approached with careful planning and dedication. Throughout this step-by-step guide, we have covered the essential aspects of launching your own car wash business. From conducting thorough market research and creating a solid business plan to setting up your workspace, procuring quality products and supplies, and implementing effective marketing strategies, you now have a comprehensive understanding of the process involved.

Remember that success in the car wash industry hinges on delivering exceptional service and building strong customer relationships. Providing top-notch customer service, continuously improving your skills and techniques, and adapting to industry trends are crucial for staying ahead of the competition and growing your business.

Additionally, maintaining a focus on financial management, pricing strategies, and profitability will ensure the long-term sustainability of your business. Keep a close eye on your expenses, track your financial performance, and adjust your pricing as needed to maximize profitability while remaining competitive in the market.

As you embark on your journey as a car wash business owner, remember to stay passionate, dedicated, and open to learning. Take advantage of networking opportunities, industry events, and continuous education to stay updated on the latest trends and techniques.

Starting a car wash business may have its challenges, but with the right mindset, proper planning, and a commitment to excellence, you have the potential to create a thriving and successful venture.

Good luck on your entrepreneurial journey, and may your car wash business achieve great success!